Get the GRADE!
AQA GCSE English
LANGUAGE

WORKBOOK

KEITH BRINDLE

The publisher would like to thank the following for permission to reproduce copyright material:

Acknowledgements: p.4: Tony Parsons: From *The Family Way* (HarperCollins, 2006); **p.5: Benjamin Zephaniah:** From *Face* (Bloomsbury, 1999); **p.6: Robert Cormier:** From *Heroes* (Puffin, 1999); **p.7: Ian Rankin:** From *Knots and Crosses* (Orion, 1999); **p.8: Clifford Simak:** From *Way Station* (Easton Press, 1963); **p.9: Mark Haddon:** From *A Spot of Bother* (Vintage, 2007); **p.11: Graham Greene:** From *The Power and the Glory* (Penguin, 1969); **p.11: Sue Townsend:** From *Rebuilding Coventry* (Methuen, 1988); **p.12: Benjamin Markovits:** From *Childish Loves* (Faber & Faber, 2012); **p.13: David Storey:** From *This Sporting Life* (Penguin, 1976); **p.14: M.L. Steadman:** From *The Light Between the Oceans* (Simon & Schuster, 2013); **p.15: Dylan Thomas:** From 'The Followers' in *Impact Two* (Heineman, 1971); **p.16: Farrukh Dhondy:** From *Come to Mecca* (Collins, 1983); **p.17: Arthur C. Clarke:** From *2001: A Space Odyssey* (Arrow, 1968); **pp.18–19, 20: Roald Dahl:** From 'Lamb to the Slaughter' in *A Roald Dahl Selection* (Penguin, 1998); **p.21: Thomas Harris:** From *The Silence of the Lambs* (Mandarin, 1991); **p.22: C.J. Sansom:** From *Dissolution* (Pan: 2003); **p.24: Katherine Mansfield:** From 'Life of Ma Parker' in *Short Stories of Our Time* (Harrap, 1985); **p. 26: William Boyd:** From *Ordinary Thunderstorms* (Bloomsbury, 2009); **p.26: Hanif Kureishi:** From *The Buddha of Suburbia* (Faber & Faber, 1990); **p.28: Isla Dewar:** From *Izzy's War* (Ebury, 2010); **p.29: Mary Lavin:** From 'The Living' in *Short Stories of Our Time* (Harrap, 1985); **p.30: Ernest Hemingway:** From *A Farewell to Arms* (Simon & Schuster, 1974); **p.32: Michael J. Hallowell:** From *Northumberland: Stories of the Supernatural* (Countryside Books: 2012); **p.33: Katie Gibbons:** From 'Police question pupil, 18, over custard pie prank', *The Times* (28 May 2014); **p.34:** From 'Ain't I a woman', *Sojourner Truth,* delivered at the Old Sojourner Women's Convention in Akron, Ohio (29 May 1851); **p.35: Eva Wiseman:** From 'The everyday fear of violence every woman has to cope with', *The Observer Magazine* (1 June 2014) Copyright Guardian News & Media Ltd 2014; **p.37: Allen Williamson:** From http://archive.joan-of-arc.org/joanofarc_short_biography.html; **p.38: Beckett and Abbott:** From *The Comic History of England* (1864); **p.40: Lynn Pan:** from 'A Decision', *Travel Writing* (Longman Imprint, 1996); **p.41: Lauren Laverne:** From 'Why are we so complacent about the play gap', *The Observer Magazine* (24 August 2014) Copyright Guardian News & Media Ltd 2014; **pp.42–3:** From http://squatchdetective.weebly.com/19th-and-early-20th-century-news-articles.html, *Naugatuck Daily News* (June 1898); **p.44: Mahatma Gandhi:** 'Quit India' speech, 8 August 1942 (Navajivan Publishing House) with permission from the publisher; **p.46: Henry Mayhew:** From 'Mayhew's London', *Impact Two* (Heinemann, 1971); **p.48: Violetta Thurstan:** From *The People Who Run: Being the tragedy of the refugees in Russia* (Penguin, 1916); **p.51: B.H. Liddell Hart** (ed.)**:** From *The Letters of Private Wheeler, 1809–1828* (The Windrush Press, 1999); **p.52: Willie Ferrie:** From a letter to 'Mama', Imperial War Museum (1918)

Photo credits: p.66 © Eric Feferberg/AFP/Getty Images; **p.72** © Monkey Business – Fotolia; **p.79** © Christopher Badzioch/E+/Getty Images

Although every effort has been made to ensure that website addresses are correct at time of going to press, Hodder Education cannot be held responsible for the content of any website mentioned. It is sometimes possible to find a relocated web page by typing in the address of the home page for a website in the URL window of your browser.

Orders: please contact Bookpoint Ltd, 130 Milton Park, Abingdon, Oxon OX14 4SB. Telephone: (44) 01235 827720. Fax: (44) 01235 400454. Lines are open 9.00–17.00, Monday to Saturday, with a 24-hour message answering service. Visit our website at www.hoddereducation.co.uk

© Keith Brindle 2015

First published in 2015 by

Hodder Education

An Hachette UK Company

338 Euston Road

London NW1 3BH

Impression number	5	4	3	2	1
Year	2019	2018	2017	2016	2015

All rights reserved. Apart from any use permitted under UK copyright law, no part of this publication may be reproduced or transmitted in any form or by any means, electronic or mechanical, including photocopying and recording, or held within any information storage and retrieval system, without permission in writing from the publisher or under licence from the Copyright Licensing Agency Limited. Further details of such licences (for reprographic reproduction) may be obtained from the Copyright Licensing Agency Limited, Saffron House, 6–10 Kirby Street, London EC1N 8TS.

Cover artwork by Jacquie Boyd at Début Art Ltd

Typeset in PMN Caecilia 11/13 by Integra Software Services Pvt. Ltd., Pondicherry, India

Printed in Spain by Graphycems

A catalogue record for this title is available from the British Library

ISBN 9781471833946

CONTENTS

Welcome to this Revision Workbook! — 1

Paper 1, Section A

About Paper 1, Section A — 3
Section As: Using evidence to support your ideas — 4
Question 1: Finding relevant details — 6
Question 2: Writing about language in literature — 10
Question 3: Dealing with structure — 16
Question 4: Character, relationships, themes and settings — 22

Paper 2, Section A

About Paper 2, Section A — 31
Question 1: Finding what is true — 32
Question 2: Dealing with two texts and summarising — 34
Question 3: Analysing persuasive language — 40
Question 4: Comparing viewpoints and writers' methods — 46

Papers 1 and 2, Section B

About the Section B questions — 55
Communicating effectively — 56
Organising your writing — 58
Vocabulary and crafting — 62
Using effective punctuation — 66
Improving sentences and grammar — 68
Writing to describe — 70
Writing to narrate — 80
Writing with a viewpoint — 90

How to revise for the English Language exam — 98
Revision checklist — 100

Welcome to this Revision Workbook!

This Revision Workbook is designed to give you practice in the essential skills that will help you improve your performance and reach the higher grades in AQA GCSE English Language. It works alongside *My Revision Notes for AQA English Language* in that it focuses on the same elements in the same order, but this Workbook gives you more opportunities to develop your abilities. Importantly, you can find answers and mark schemes at (www.hoddereducation.co.uk/myrevisionnotes/gcse-english-language), so as you go along you can see how you are doing – and learn how to do even better.

What exactly must I do?

Fortunately, the exam is very predictable.
- It consists of two papers.
- Each paper lasts 1 hour and 45 minutes.
- The questions will always be 'the same'.

Paper 1

There will be four questions based on an extract from a modern novel.
The questions will be as follows:

Section A: Reading

Q1	4 marks	You will have to find four details in the first part of the text and list them.
Q2	8 marks	This is the language question. You will be asked how the writer uses language for a particular purpose – perhaps to set the scene – in the section of text.
Q3	8 marks	This question is on the structure of the text: how the writer has organised the writing.
Q4	20 marks	This question will ask you how the writer has created a particular impression – of the characters, or the setting or whatever – and how you feel about what you have read.

Section B: Writing

Q5/Q6	40 marks	You will answer one question from the two offered: there will be two tasks asking you to describe **or** two asking you to narrate **or** one of each.

Paper 2

Again there will be four questions, but in this case they will be based on two non-fiction sources. The questions will be as follows:

Section A: Reading

Q1	4 marks	You will be given eight statements about a section of one of the texts: you have to shade in boxes to say which four are true.
Q2	8 marks	You will need to write about both texts and summarise some element of their differences or similarities.
Q3	12 marks	Focusing on just one of the texts, you will have to say how the writer has used language for effect.
Q4	16 marks	You have to consider both texts again and this time compare their ideas or attitudes – for example, the attitudes of the writers towards a person or a place; but you must also compare the methods they use to present their ideas and attitudes.

Section B: Writing

Q5	40 marks	You will have to give your point of view on some topic connected to the material in Section A.

About Paper 1, Section A

This section tests your reading of fiction. You will be presented with an extract that is about a page long, and you will be asked four questions about it. It will be a modern text – from the twentieth or twenty-first centuries.

What, exactly, must I do?

It is recommended that you spend an hour answering the questions in Section A – although, of course, you have to read the text in that time as well.

If it takes you about 10 minutes to read the text carefully, and to have a quick look at the questions and what is expected of you, it means you will need to complete:

- Question 1 (4 marks) in 4 or 5 minutes.
- Question 2 (8 marks) in 8 or 9 minutes.
- Question 3 (8 marks) in 8 or 9 minutes.
- Question 4 (20 marks) in 20 or 21 minutes.

Apart from Question 1, when you will be listing details, you will be expected to support your ideas with relevant quotations throughout.

Candidates who reach the higher grades will demonstrate the ability to make points, support them with the right evidence and then offer analysis of the text. That means giving alternative interpretations and linking relevant points.

There are no marks for spelling, sentences or punctuation on this section, but the more clearly you can express yourself, the easier it will be for the examiner to understand and reward your efforts.

Section As: Using evidence to support your ideas

When responding to the questions in Section A of both papers – apart from the initial question – you will be expected to support your ideas with quotations from the texts.

What, exactly, must I do?

It is relatively simple:
- Find the necessary words or phrases to prove what you are saying.
- Identify them in your answer by putting them inside quotation marks.

If you can embed quotations – that is, put them within sentences so that the sentences continue to flow on – it can be more impressive.

Read this extract.

'Your parents ruin the first half of your life,' Cat's mother told her when she was eleven years old, 'and your children ruin the second half.'

It was said with the smallest of smiles, like one of those jokes that are not really a joke at all.

Cat was an exceptionally bright child, and she wanted to examine this proposition. How exactly had she ruined her mother's life? But there was no time. Her mother was in a hurry to get out of there. The black cab was waiting.

One of Cat's sisters was crying – maybe even both of them. But that wasn't the concern of Cat's mother. Because inside the waiting cab there was a man who loved her, and who no doubt made her feel good about herself, and who surely made her feel as though there was an un-ruined life out there for her somewhere, probably beyond the door of the rented flat in St John's Wood.

(Tony Parsons, *The Family Way*)

1 Write in a quotation to support each point being made below.

Remember to put quotation marks around the words you select.

- We suspect that Cat's mother does not have a positive view of family life, because she says: ....

....

- Of course, Cat's mother could have been joking, since we are told: ....

....

- We do know for certain, however, that Cat is very intelligent, since the writer describes her as: ....

....

- We also know this because the very 'grown up' language the writer uses makes us think that these are exactly the words in Cat's mind: ....

....

Section As: Using evidence to support your ideas

- The reader understands Cat's confusion when we are given the question that is inside her head: ....

2 Embed quotations in the following sentences.

- Cat's sisters were clearly not happy, ...

  but we are told, ...

  which makes her sound heartless. She simply leaves.

- It sounds as though she cares most about herself, since she is going to meet ....

  ....

  Presumably she manages just to forget about her children.

3 Write one or two additional sentences about Cat's mother, based on the final lines of the extract. Support what you say with quotations; embed some if you can.

....

....

....

....

Extended practice

This extract is about a boy who has been in a car crash and has suffered severe damage to his face.

> After a week at home, Martin made a return visit to the hospital with his parents to see Dr Owens and Alan Green. Between them they had made some important decisions. There were to be no more operations. Martin had made up his mind: he'd had all the surgery he required and he wasn't going to have repeated stays in hospital trying to achieve a perfect face. He was thankful that there wasn't any rebuilding to be done and that the newly grafted skin had begun to settle in. The very rough areas were now covered with new skin, and the scars where the old met the new were less prominent. But Martin was still looking into mirrors at every opportunity, which worried Alan Green.
>
> 'Listen, Martin,' Alan said, 'looking in the mirror with confidence is great, but don't spend too much time doing it. Simply treat mirrors as you did before the operation.'
>
> His mother turned to Alan with a knowing smile. 'Even before the accident he spent a lot of time looking in mirrors.'
>
> (Benjamin Zephaniah, *Face*)

What do we learn about Martin here? Support what you say with quotations.

Answer on lined paper.

Q1: Finding relevant details

Paper 1, Question 1 is likely to be based on the first 10 or so lines of the text that will be used for all four questions in Paper 1. You will have to **find four things** – perhaps about a person in the text, or about the situation or the setting. You can quote the details or put them into your own words.

There are 4 marks for this question and you will need to complete it in 4 or 5 minutes.

What, exactly, must I do?

There is no need to write at length. All you have to do is list four relevant points. If they are not direct quotations, there must be evidence for them in the text.

1 List four things we learn about Nicole Renard in this extract.

Our teacher swept into the classroom, followed by the most beautiful girl I had ever seen.

Nicole Renard was small and slender, with shining black hair that fell to her shoulders. The pale purity of her face reminded me of the statue of St Therese in St Jude's Church. As she looked modestly down at the floor, our eyes met and a flash of recognition passed between us, as if we had known each other before. Something else flashed in her eyes, too, a hint of mischief as if she were telling me we were going to have good times together.

(Robert Cormier, *Heroes*)

1 ....

2 ....

3 ....

4 ....

Read this text.

On the steps of the Great London Road police station in Edinburgh, John Rebus lit his last cigarette of the day before pushing open the imposing door and stepping inside.

The station was old, its floor dark and marbled. It had about it the fading grandeur of a dead aristocracy. It had character.

Rebus waved to the duty sergeant, who was tearing old pictures from the notice-board and pinning up new ones in their place. He climbed the great curving staircase to his office. Campbell was just leaving.

'Hello, John.'

McGregor Campbell, a Detective Sergeant like Rebus, was donning hat and coat.

Rebus began checking the messages on his desk.

(Ian Rankin, *Knots and Crosses*)

2 List four things we learn about the police station here.

1 ....

....

2 ....

....

3 ....

....

4 ....

....

3 List four things we learn about Rebus.

1 ....

....

2 ....

....

3 ....

....

4 ....

....

Read this extract, about people on a farm.

There had been a winter night and he had been, it seemed, no more than three or four. His mother was busy at the stove with supper. He was sitting on the floor in the centre of the kitchen, playing with some blocks, and outside he could hear the muffled howling of the wind as it prowled along the eaves. His father had come in from milking in the barn, and a gust of wind and a swirl of snow had come into the room with him. Then he'd shut the door and the wind and snow were gone, shut outside this house, condemned to the wilderness of night. His father had set the pail of milk that he had been carrying on the kitchen sink and Enoch saw that his beard and eyebrows were coated with snow and there was frost on the whiskers all around his mouth.

(Clifford Simak, *Way Station*)

4 List four things we know about the weather here.

1 ....

....

2 ....

....

3 ....

....

4 ....

....

5 List four things we know about the members of the family.

1 ....

....

2 ....

....

3 ....

....

4 ....

....

Paper 1, Q1: Finding relevant details

Extended practice

Here, a woman has persuaded her husband – who thinks he might be dying – to visit the doctor.

Jean booked an appointment and drove George to the surgery.

It was not something she was looking forward to. But Katie was right. It was best to take the bull by the horns.

She put him through his paces in the car. He was to tell Dr Barghoutian the truth. None of this nonsense about sunstroke or coming over light-headed. He was not to leave until Dr Barghoutian had promised to do something. And he was to tell her afterwards exactly what Dr Barghoutian had said.

She reminded him that Katie's wedding was coming up and that if he wasn't there to give his daughter away and make a speech, then he was going to have some explaining to do.

They sat next to one another in the waiting room. She tried to chat, but he was more interested in an elderly copy of *OK!* magazine.

When his name was called she patted him gently on the leg to wish him luck. He made his way across the room, stooping a little and keeping his eyes fixed firmly on the carpet.

(Mark Haddon, *A Spot of Bother*)

- List four things we learn about Jean. (Do not include information from the introductory sentence.)

    1 ....

    2 ....

    3 ....

    4 ....

- List four things we learn about George. (Do not include information from the introductory sentence.)

    1 ....

    2 ....

    3 ....

    4 ....

Q2: Writing about language in literature

In Paper 1, Question 2 you will have to write about **how language has been used** in a section of the fiction text. There are 8 marks available and you should allow 8 or 9 minutes to answer the question.

What, exactly, must I do?

You will be directed to a section of the text – perhaps up to about 10 lines – and told to write about how the writer, in those lines, has used:

- words and phrases
- language features and techniques
- sentence forms.

The key word is '**how**'. You will be discussing the effect or effects on the reader: what the language suggests and **how** that effect is achieved.

1 How has the language been used in each of these examples?
   Explain the effect that is being created by each of the techniques. In each case, say what reaction the reader is expected to have.

- 'He was like a broken wheel.'

   This simile suggests: ....

   ....

- 'His heart had shattered and his life was in pieces.'

   ....

   ....

   ....

- 'Tortured and tormented, through the night he moaned, wept and wailed.'

   ....

   ....

   ....

- 'His family was dead. No one had survived. They were not living, smiling and joking; they were buried and gone. And how would he cope?'

   ....

   ....

   ....

Paper 1, Q2: Writing about language in literature

This extract is set in Mexico.

> He stood stiffly in the shade, a small man dressed in a shabby dark city suit, carrying a small briefcase. His bloodshot eyes looked slyly out of their corners at Mr Tench.

(Graham Greene, *The Power and the Glory*)

2 What is the effect of the language here? How are we supposed to react to the following?

- 'stiffly' ....
- 'shabby dark city suit' ....
- 'bloodshot eyes' ....
- 'slyly' ....

Read this extract.

> My parents are not good-looking. My father looks like a tennis ball and my mother closely resembles a bread knife.
>
> I love my brother Sidney, and I think he loves me. He is married to a sad woman called Ruth. Ruth sighs before she speaks, and when she has finished speaking she sighs again. Sighs are her punctuation marks.
>
> Sidney is successful because, like me, he is beautiful. Customers are hypnotised by the deep brown of his eyes.

(Sue Townsend, *Rebuilding Coventry*)

3 What impression of these people is being created?
Complete this table. Try to offer more than one explanation when you can.

Phrase	Literary technique	Explanation of effect
'like a tennis ball'	Simile	This suggests the father has no hair or very little hair and…
'closely resembles a bread knife'		
'Sighs are her punctuation marks'		
'hypnotised by the deep brown of his eyes'		

11

In this extract, the narrator is describing a teacher with whom he worked.

> Many of my colleagues, especially the older ones, treated him the way you might treat a homeless man on the subway. Not unkindly, but with the deference you might show to someone who isn't particularly clean. Cleanliness, in fact, was never Peter's strong suit. He always wore the same black chalk-stained smoking jacket to class; and his beard, which was both wild and sparse, was larded in the morning with crumbs of his breakfast and stained in the afternoon by the grease of his lunch. But if he smelled of anything, it was the sweetness of pipe tobacco.

(Benjamin Markovits, *Childish Loves*)

4 What is suggested about Peter in the following words and phrases? What do they make the reader think about him? Try to give more than one interpretation in each case.

- 'treated him in the way you might treat a homeless man on the subway'

....

....

- 'deference you might show to someone who isn't particularly clean'

....

....

....

- 'chalk-stained smoking jacket'

....

....

- 'his beard ... was both wild and sparse'

....

....

- 'larded ... with crumbs of his breakfast'

....

....

- 'stained ... by the grease of his lunch'

....

....

- 'sweetness of pipe tobacco'

....

....

Here, a young man goes for a trial at his local Rugby League club:

> When I ran on to the field it was almost dark. A heavy mist hung over the valley and enclosed the ground in a tight grey wall of drizzle. It was bitterly cold. The players ran around in groups, small and unreal beneath the half-empty flanks of the terraces; insects released on a space. I felt sick and frightened. Everything outside the dark wreath of the crowd and the wooden pinnacles of the stadium was hidden. We were isolated in the shell of the stands.
>
> (David Storey, *This Sporting Life*)

5 What word/words or phrases could you use to describe the mood in this scene?

....

....

6 How does the language establish the atmosphere? To answer, decide what impression we get from the following words and phrases. (Make sure you identify the metaphors as you present your explanations.)

- 'A heavy mist hung over the valley'

....

....

....

- 'enclosed the ground'

....

....

- 'a tight grey wall of drizzle'

....

....

....

- 'bitterly'

....

....

- 'unreal'

....

....

AQA GCSE English Language Workbook

- 'insects released on a space'

....

....

- 'dark wreath of the crowd'

....

....

- 'We were isolated in the shell of the stands'

....

....

....

7 What is the effect of the short sentences here? (e.g. 'It was bitterly cold' and 'I felt sick and frightened'.)

....

....

....

Consider how the writer uses language differently in this extract.

> As Tom walks down the path, he snaps off a yellow bud from one of the rose bushes Isabel planted when they first moved here. Its fragrance is already strong, and takes him back almost two decades to the picture of her, kneeling in the freshly dug bed, hands pressing down the earth around the young bush. 'We've finally got our rose garden, Tom,' she had said. It was the first time he had seen her smile since she had left Partaguese, and the image stayed with him, as clear as a photograph.
>
> There is a small gathering at the church hall after the funeral. Tom stays as long as politeness demands. But he wishes the people really knew who they were mourning: the Isabel he had met on the jetty, so full of life and daring and mischief. His Izzy. His other half of the sky.

(M.L. Stedman, *The Light Between Oceans*)

8 Why are longer, complex sentences used to tell us about his memories of Isabel in the first paragraph?

....

....

....

9 What is the effect of the sentence that includes a list of three? ('But he wishes…')

....

....

....

10 Comment on the effect of:

- the simile: 'as clear as a photograph'

....

....

....

- the metaphor: 'his other half of the sky'.

....

....

....

Extended practice

The scene here is much busier.

It was six o'clock on a winter's evening. Thin, dingy rain spat and drizzled past the lighted street lamps. The pavements shone long and yellow. With overcoat collars turned up and bowlers and trilbies weeping, youngish men from the offices bundled home against the thistly wind; and older men, clinging to the big, black circular birds of their umbrellas, were wafted back, up the hills, to safe, hot slippered, weather-proof hearths, and wives called Mother, and old, fond, fleabag dogs, and the radio babbling.

(Dylan Thomas, 'The Followers')

How does the language here bring the scene to life? Write about how the writer has used:

- words and phrases
- language features and techniques
- sentence forms.

Answer on lined paper.

Q3: Dealing with structure

Paper 1, Question 3 will ask you **how the writer has structured the text** to interest the reader. You need to write about features such as the opening, how the text develops and perhaps how it ends; and about how the writer has used techniques such as shifts of perspective, speech, repetition, change of focus, extended imagery, and perhaps particular vocabulary and sentence structures. There are 8 marks for this question and you will need to complete your answer in 8 or 9 minutes.

What, exactly, must I do?

You need to consider the whole of the source, so resist the temptation to deal only with the opening section. Think about how the source begins, but also where it ends and how it has got there. Look out for elements such as those mentioned in the adjacent box – these are merely examples, though, and there might well be other methods employed.

Read this text.

There was a short route home from school and the long route. Jolil took the long route because by the time he got out of school the other boys who lived in his building had gone home. Mr Morrison had kept him behind in his office and shown him some books.

'We must do something about your English,' Mr Morrison had said. 'Come up to my room at ten to four and we'll go over some things together.'

Jolil didn't want to refuse. He didn't want to tell Mr Morrison why he was impatient to get home. He usually left by the school gate with five or six of the other Asian boys. It wasn't planned, but it was necessary. If they walked home together, they could pass the gangs of older white boys who gathered outside the school gates without fear. They'd take the short route home, and if they passed the cluster of hostile faces outside the white estate at the end of their street, they could quicken their steps and feel the safe warmth of being part of a crowd. If you walked alone, you walked along the Whitechapel Road and came round to the flats the long way.

'I got something out of the public library especially for you, Jolil,' Mr Morrison said, and he handed Jolil a book on the martial arts. He had told Mr Morrison some days before that that was what he was interested in.

'Don't just stare at the pictures, try and read some of it,' Mr Morrison said.

(Farrukh Dhondy, *Come to Mecca*)

1 How do these paragraphs build an impression of Jolil's life and what he is like?

....

....

....

....

2 Why, do you think, does it begin with mention of the long route and the short route?

....

....

....

....

3 What might be the significance of the book on martial arts?

....

....

....

....

4 How do the words of Mr Morrison add to the story and suggest what might be to come?

....

....

....

....

....

This is from a novel that begins in another time.

> The drought had lasted now for ten million years, and the reign of the terrible lizards had long since ended. Here on the Equator, in the continent which would one day be known as Africa, the battle for existence had reached a new climax of ferocity, and the visitor was not yet in sight. In this barren and desiccated land, only the small or the swift or the fierce could flourish, or even hope to survive.
>
> The man-apes of the veldt were none of these things, and they were not flourishing; indeed, they were already far down the road to racial extinction. About fifty of them occupied a group of caves overlooking a small, parched valley, which was divided by a sluggish stream fed from snows in the mountains two hundred miles to the north. In bad times, the stream vanished completely, and the tribe lived in the shadow of thirst.
>
> It was always hungry, and now it was starving. When the first glow of dawn crept into the cave, Moon-Watcher saw that his father had died in the night. He did not know that the Old One was his father, for such a relationship was utterly beyond his understanding, but as he looked at the emaciated body he felt a dim disquiet that was the ancestor of sadness.
>
> (Arthur C. Clarke, *2001: A Space Odyssey*)

AQA GCSE English Language Workbook

5 How does the writer engage the reader's attention in the first sentence?

....

....

....

....

6 How is the idea of a 'barren' land extended through the extract?

....

....

....

....

7 How does the writer move the perspective from a very general description down to a more personal view?

....

....

....

....

8 Why is the phrase 'ancestor of sadness' especially relevant at the end?

....

....

....

....

Read this opening to a short story.

> The room was warm and clean, the curtains drawn, the two table lamps alight – hers and the one by the empty chair opposite. On the sideboard behind her, two tall glasses, soda water, whisky. Fresh ice cubes in the Thermos bucket.
>
> Mary Maloney was waiting for Patrick, her husband, a detective, to come home from work.

Paper 1, Q3: Dealing with structure

Now and again she would glance up at the clock, but without anxiety, merely to please herself with the thought that each minute gone by made it nearer the time when he would come home. There was a slow smiling air about her, and about everything she did. The drop of the head as she bent over her sewing was curiously tranquil. Her skin – for this was her sixth month with child – had acquired a wonderful shining quality, the mouth was soft, and the eyes, with their new placid look, seemed larger, darker than before.

(Roald Dahl, 'Lamb to the Slaughter')

9 How do we know immediately that someone is coming?

....

....

....

....

10 What is the effect of the minor (incomplete) sentences in the first paragraph?

....

....

....

....

11 'There was a slow smiling air about her': what is the mood in the final paragraph and how is it presented?

....

....

....

....

....

12 'The eyes … seemed larger, darker than before': What is the effect of these final words and how is the effect different from what has gone before?

....

....

....

....

The story continues: When Patrick arrives, he tells his wife he is leaving her. She hits him with a frozen leg of lamb, and crushes his skull. She then puts the meat in the oven to cook, to hide the evidence, and calls the police. She says someone has murdered him. When they have finished their initial investigations, she invites them to eat the meal she has been cooking.

This is how the story ends:

> Mrs Maloney listened to them through the open door, and she could hear them speaking among themselves, their voices thick and sloppy because their mouths were full of meat.
>
> 'Have some more, Charlie?'
>
> 'No. Better not finish it.'
>
> 'She wants us to finish it. She said so. Be doing her a favour.'
>
> 'Okay then. Give me some more.'
>
> 'That's a hell of a big club the guy must've used to hit poor Patrick,' one of them was saying. 'The doc says his skull was smashed all to pieces just like from a sledge-hammer.'
>
> 'That's why it ought to be easy to find. Whoever done it, they're not going to be carrying a thing like that around with them longer than they need.'
>
> One of them belched.
>
> 'Personally, I think it's right here on the premises.'
>
> 'Probably right under our very noses. What do you think, Jack?'
>
> And in the other room, Mary Maloney started to giggle.

(Roald Dahl, 'Lamb to the Slaughter')

13 How do the adjectives 'thick and sloppy' add to the horror?

....

....

14 Why is the sentence 'Be doing her a favour' ironic?

....

....

15 Why is the sentence 'One of them belched' so unpleasant?

....

....

16 In what ways are the final two lines an effective ending to the story?

....

....

....

....

Paper 1, Q3: Dealing with structure

Extended practice

In this extract, Clarice Starling, who works for the FBI, has gone to try to get information from Dr Hannibal Lecter. He is a difficult man to deal with. He is extremely intelligent but dangerous, and is locked in an asylum because he is a cannibal.

Descending through the asylum towards the most secure area, Starling managed to shut out much of the slammings and the screaming, though she felt them shiver the air against her skin. Pressure built on her as though she sank through water, down and down.

The proximity of madmen braced Starling for her job. But she needed more than resolution. She needed to be calm, to be still. She had to use patience in the face of the awful need to hurry. If Dr Lecter knew the answer, she'd have to find it down among the tendrils of his thought.

A big orderly opened the last door for her. The corridor between the cells was dim. Near the far end she could see bright light from the last cell shining on the corridor floor.

'Dr Lecter's awake,' she said.

'Yes. Stay in the middle going down, don't touch the bars, right?'

Starling went down the long corridor alone. She did not look into the cells on either side. Her footfalls seemed loud to her. The only other sounds were snoring from one cell, maybe two, and a low chuckle from another.

She didn't want to look into Dr Lecter's cell until she was sure he had seen her. She passed it, feeling itchy between the shoulders.

Dr Lecter wore the white asylum pyjamas in his white cell. The only colours in the cell were his hair and eyes and his red mouth, in a face so long out of the sun it leached into the surrounding whiteness, his features seemed suspended above the collar of his shirt. He sat at this table behind the nylon net that kept him back from the bars. He was sketching, using his hand for a model. As she watched, he turned his hand over and, flexing his fingers to great tension, drew the inside of his forearm.

She came a little closer to the bars, and he looked up. For Starling, every shadow in the cell flew into his eyes.

'Good evening, Dr Lecter.'

The tip of his tongue appeared, with his lips equally red. It touched his upper lip in the exact centre and went back in again.

'Clarice.'

She heard the slight metallic rasp behind his voice and wondered how long it had been since last he spoke. Beats of silence...

(Thomas Harris, *The Silence of the Lambs*)

How has the writer structured the text to interest you as a reader?

You could write about:

- what the writer focuses your attention on at the beginning
- how and why the writer develops and shifts this focus as the extract develops
- any other structural features that interest you.

Write your answer on lined paper.

Q4: Character, relationships, themes and settings

Question 4 will ask you about the **impressions created** by the writer – perhaps of a character, of characters' relationships, of a theme, setting or event. You will be expected to say what impressions have been created and how successfully they have been presented, which means you must **evaluate** the way the writer has done it and say why the piece of writing is effective.

There are 20 marks for this question, so you will need to answer it in 20 minutes or just over.

What, exactly, must I do?

You will probably be directed to look at just a section of the source material – so make sure you include material only from that section. Your answer will be assessed on three skills:

- your ability to write about the impressions
- your ability to judge how the writer has created these impressions
- how well you support your opinions with quotations.

This passage is from a novel set in 1537.

As I approached London Bridge, I averted my eyes from the arch, where the heads of those executed for treason stood on their long poles, the gulls circling and pecking. I have never welcomed such sights and do not enjoy even the bear baiting.

The great bridge was thronged with people as usual; many of the merchant classes were in mourning black for Queen Jane, who had died of childbed fever two weeks before. Tradesfolk cried their wares from the shops on the ground floors of the buildings, built so closely upon it they looked as though they might topple into the river at any moment. On the upper storeys, women were hauling in their washing, for clouds were now darkening the sky from the west. Gossiping and calling to each other, they put me in mind, in my miserable mood, of crows cawing in a great tree.

(C.J. Sansom, *Dissolution*)

1 What impressions do you get of London and its people? List your ideas.
  Try not just to list facts, but to interpret them: say what the facts suggest about the city and those who live there.

- ....
  ....
- ....
  ....
- ....
  ....
- ....
  ....
- ....
  ....

Paper 1, Q4: Character, relationships, themes and settings

2. What methods has the writer used to try to make the description interesting? List them, with brief quotations. Consider the use of verbs, the use of specific detail, the sentences, the mentions of the birds, the weather, the overall mood.

- ....
- ....
- ....
- ....
- ....
- ....
- ....
- ....
- ....
- ....
- ....

3. List some words or phrases you might use to evaluate how impressions have been created in any text:

- 'This clearly suggests…'
- 'The reader immediately thinks…'
- 'This is effective because…'

- ....
- ....
- ....
- ....
- ....
- ....
- ....
- ....

AQA GCSE English Language Workbook

4 Complete this table.

Phrase	Explanation of how successfully it works
'I averted my eyes'	The verb 'averted' immediately makes us think he cannot bear to look and suggests he is appalled by what he sees.
'the gulls circling and pecking'	
'thronged'	
'mourning black'	
'clouds were now darkening the sky from the west'	
'gossiping and calling to each other'	
'crows cawing in a great tree'	

Consider this opening:

> When the literary gentleman, whose flat old Ma Parker cleaned every Tuesday, opened the door to her that morning, he asked after her grandson. Ma Parker stood on the door-mat inside the dark little hall, and she stretched out her hand to help her gentleman shut the door before she replied. 'We buried 'im yesterday, sir,' she said quietly.
>
> 'Oh, dear me! I'm sorry to hear that,' said the literary gentleman in a shocked tone. He was in the middle of his breakfast. He wore a shabby dressing-gown and carried a crumpled newspaper in one hand. But he felt awkward. He could hardly go back to the sitting-room without saying something – something more. Then, because these people set such store by funerals he said kindly, 'I hope the funeral went off all right.'
>
> 'Beg parding, sir?' said old Ma Parker huskily.
>
> Poor old bird! Ma Parker gave no answer. She bent her head and hobbled off to the kitchen. The literary gentleman raised his eyebrows and went back to his breakfast.
>
> (Katherine Mansfield, 'Life of Ma Parker')

Paper 1, Q4: Character, relationships, themes and settings

Question: 'This extract gives a very clear impression of the differences between these two people.' To what extent do you agree?

In your response, you should:
- Write about your own impressions of the characters.
- Evaluate how the writer has created these impressions.
- Support your opinions with quotations from the text.

5 Here is part of a response to this question. Fill in the gaps.

```
It is clear from the start that the two people are very different,
because she is called '.................................................................' (quotation).
This makes her sound as if ................................................. (explanation).

The man is not given a name — he is just '.................................
..................' (quotation), which makes him seem ..................................
.............................. (explanation). She is much more common. The writer
................................................. (evaluation) in the way Ma Parker speaks.
She misses a consonant (''im') and says, '.........................................'
(quotation), which isn't even Standard English and also gets the wrong
word. The writer ................................................. (evaluation).

The literary gentleman, in contrast, is intentionally made to sound very
formal and old-fashioned: '.................................................................' (quotation).
When he speaks in 'a shocked tone', the writer could be implying that
he is trying to react in a decent way — though, in fact, his thoughts
are actually elsewhere: '.................................................................' (quotation).
```

6 Complete your answer to the question, remembering to include the impressions created and the methods used, with quotations to support what you say and some evaluation of the writer's success.
You might want to mention why the writer includes:
- Old Ma Parker's role in the flat
- Ma Parker standing on the doormat and helping him to shut the door
- 'she said quietly', 'said old Ma Parker huskily'
- 'these people'
- 'I hope the funeral went off all right.'
- 'kindly'
- 'Poor old bird!'
- how the scene ends.

....

....

....

Continue on lined paper.

25

This passage is about a man 'on the run' from the police.

'£100,000 REWARD FOR INFORMATION leading to the arrest of Adam Kindred.' Adam regarded the full-page advertisement in the newspaper with frank astonishment and an obscure, though fleeting, sense of pride. Never had he seen his name written so large – and to be worth a £100,000 reward. Who would have thought it? There was his picture, also, and details of his height, weight and race. Adam Kindred, 31, white male, English, dark hair. His raincoat and briefcase were also specified as if he never wore or carried anything else. Then the reality of the situation struck him and he felt shame creep over him, imagining his family seeing this, imagining people who had known him, speculating. Adam Kindred, a murderer…?

(William Boyd, *Ordinary Thunderstorms*)

7 Look specifically at the sentence types in this passage. How successfully has the writer used them to show how Adam Kindred is thinking?

....
....
....
....
....
....
....
....
....
....

Read this extract:

Anwar was sitting on a bed in the living room, which wasn't his normal bed in its normal place. He was wearing a frayed and mouldy-looking pyjama jacket, and I noticed that his toenails rather resembled cashew nuts. For some reason his mouth was hanging open and he was panting, though he couldn't have run for a bus in the last five minutes. He was unshaven, and thinner than I'd ever seen him. His lips were dry and flaking. His skin looked yellow and his eyes were sunken, each of them seeming to lie in a bruise. Next to the bed was a dirty encrusted pot with a pool of urine in it. I'd never seen anyone dying before, but I was sure Anwar qualified. Anwar was staring at my steaming kebab as though it were a torture instrument. I chewed speedily to get rid of it.

'Why didn't you tell me he's sick?' I whispered to Jamila.

(Hanif Kureishi, *The Buddha of Suburbia*)

Paper 1, Q4: Character, relationships, themes and settings

8 Evaluate how well the descriptive details have been used here to give the impression that Anwar is sick.

This is the opening of a novel set in the 1930s.

> There was rapture in Izzy's life. It came when she was flying, when she had such a view – God's view, her father called it. Well, he would. She thought she could write a book about the things she'd seen from above: herds of deer, hundreds of them rippling across the hilltops. She saw houses, gardens; washing flapping on the line; people small as matchstick men, moving through streets and stopping, sometimes, to look up at her hovering above them, and point. Once, she'd seen a couple entangled in their own not-as-private-as-they-thought rapture on a sun-soaked moor. She saw the shape and glide of the rivers, was shoulder to shoulder with mountains. It took her breath away. She was addicted to the air. Removed from earthly worries and demands, she was truly happy.

(Isla Dewar, *Izzy's War*)

9 How well does the writer present Izzy's excitement?
Consider:
- the details mentioned
- Izzy's feelings
- the methods used by the writer.

Try to evaluate how successfully the writer has presented the excitement.

Paper 1, Q4: Character, relationships, themes and settings

Here, two boys are talking.

'How many dead people do you know?' said Mickser suddenly.

Immediately, painfully, I felt my answer would show me once more inferior to him. He was eight and I was a year younger. 'Do you mean ghosts?' I said slowly, to gain time.

We were sitting one on each post of the big gate at the schoolhouse that was down on the main road.

'No,' said Mickser, 'I mean corpses.'

'But don't they get buried?' I cried.

'They're not buried for three days,' said Mickser scathingly. 'They have to be scrubbed and laid out. You're not allowed to keep them any longer than that though, because their eyes go like this,' and he put his hands up to his eyes and drew down the lower lids to show the inner lids with swimming watery blood. 'They rot,' he explained.

(Mary Lavin, 'The Living')

10 'The writer presents two totally convincing children.' To what extent do you agree? Evaluate the success of the presentation by analysing what they do, what they say and how they say it.

Extended practice

The narrator here is an ambulance man working in Italy in World War I. A shell has exploded where he and his colleagues were eating.

> I heard close to me someone saying, 'Mamma mia! Oh, mamma mia!' I pulled and twisted and got my legs loose finally and turned round and touched him. It was Passini and when I touched him he screamed. His legs were towards me and I saw that they were both smashed above the knee. One leg was gone and the other was held by tendons and part of the trouser, and the stump twitched and jerked as though it were not connected. He bit his arm and moaned 'Oh, mamma mia, mamma mia. Oh, Jesus, shoot me. Stop it. Stop it. Stop it. Mamma mia.' Then he was quiet, biting his arm, the stump of his leg twitching.
>
> I tried to get close to him to get a tourniquet on the legs but I could not move. I tried again and my legs moved a little. Passini was quiet now. I saw that there was no need to try to help him, because he was dead already. I made sure he was dead. I sat up straight and as I did so something inside my head moved like the weights on a doll's eyes and it hit me inside my eyeballs. My legs felt warm and wet and my shoes were wet and warm inside. I knew that I was hit and leaned over and put my hand on my knee. My knee wasn't there.

(Ernest Hemingway, *A Farewell to Arms*)

Task: 'The writer makes this event horribly real.' To what extent do you agree?
In your response, you should:

- Write about your impressions of the scene.
- Evaluate how the writer has created these impressions.
- Support your opinions with quotations from the text.

Continue on lined paper if necessary.

About Paper 2, Section A

Paper 2, Section A is challenging because you have to deal with two texts on a similar subject – one from the nineteenth century and one from the twentieth or twenty-first centuries. They will be non-fiction, so they could be diary entries, letters, articles, reports, etc.
It is especially important that you do not panic about the nineteenth-century extract. Even if some of the language or ideas are tricky, read it slowly and carefully and it will begin to make sense.

What, exactly, must I do?

You are advised to spend approximately one hour on the section, reading the texts and answering the questions. If you commit approximately 15 minutes to reading the texts carefully, that will leave you 45 minutes to write your answers.

As with Paper 1, Section A, there are 40 marks available. After reading the two texts, you will have to use the rest of your time wisely and appropriately.

- Question 1 (4 marks) – spend 4 or 5 minutes.
- Question 2 (8 marks) – spend 8 or 9 minutes.
- Question 3 (12 marks) – spend 12 or 13 minutes.
- Question 4 (16 marks) – spend 16 or 17 minutes.

Question 1 is multiple choice, so you will be shading in boxes to indicate the things that are true. For the other questions in Section A you will be expected to support your ideas with relevant quotations throughout.

Once again, there are no marks for your technical accuracy, but you should try to be as accurate as possible to help the examiner understand the points you are making. If the examiner finds your English confused or confusing, or if they can't read your handwriting, it is difficult for them to reward you highly.

Q1: Finding what is true

Paper 2, Question 1 is likely to be based on the first 15 or 20 lines of one of the two non-fiction sources you will be dealing with in this paper. You will be given **eight statements** and will have to decide which **four are true**. Since this is multiple choice, you need simply to shade in the boxes beside the true statements. There are 4 marks for this question and you will need to complete it in 4 or 5 minutes.

What, exactly, must I do?

Read through the list of statements, locate the relevant section in the text for each and then decide whether the statement you have been given is correct. You will need to read carefully and think clearly because you might well be dealing with implicit ideas as well as explicit information.

This passage is from a book about ghosts.

People who visit ancient sites may actually find themselves transported through time and able to witness events which occurred hundreds or even thousands of years ago. The Treasury House in York, for example, is famous for producing a 'time slip' involving Roman soldiers who were once stationed there. Engineer Harry Martindale had one of the most terrifying encounters of all there. Whilst working on his own in the cellar, Harry was astonished to hear a trumpet call. Then, to his amazement, a solid figure in Roman military dress 'walked out of the wall' in front of him. The apparition was that of a soldier wearing a tunic and carrying a round shield. Terrified, Harry ran to the corner of the cellar and cowered down, watching in astonishment as the first figure was then followed by an officer on horseback and a procession of legionaries.

As this procession walked through the cellar, Harry noticed that they were only visible from the thigh upwards. It was as if the legionaries were walking on a surface at least two feet below the current level of the cellar floor. It is now known that a road did, indeed, exist directly underneath the Treasury House. Intriguingly, sceptics poured scorn on Harry's story, arguing that Roman legionaries did not carry circular shields. However, at least one legion stationed at York was supported by auxiliary units, and these auxiliaries did carry circular or oval shields!

(Michael J. Hallowell, *Northumberland: Stories of the Supernatural*)

Choose **four** statements below that are TRUE.

- Shade the boxes of the ones you think are true
- Choose a maximum of four statements.

A If you visit an ancient site, you will see Roman soldiers. ☐
B More than one person has seen Roman soldiers in the Treasury House. ☐
C Harry Martindale had a frightening experience in the Treasury House. ☐
D Someone shouted to Harry while he was in the cellar. ☐
E The Roman soldier who Harry saw was wearing only a tunic. ☐
F The soldiers were walking on their knees. ☐
G Some people did not believe Harry's story. ☐
H Some soldiers in York did have round shields. ☐

Extended practice

This extract is from a newspaper.

An end-of-term prank backfired for a grammar school boy who has been expelled and questioned by police for hurling a custard pie at his teacher.

Jacob Dowdle, 18, was celebrating his last day of lessons when he threw a paper plate topped with whipped cream into the face of his female head of year at Altrincham Grammar School in Cheshire.

Police then visited the teenager at his home and questioned him on suspicion of common assault after the teacher complained that her eyes had been damaged. Mr Dowdle has been expelled from the all-boys school after posting a video of the incident on Facebook. It has since been removed.

The A Level student said that he was full of remorse and had written a letter of apology to the teacher, which he claims has remained unanswered. He has criticised the school for reacting in a way that could damage his university applications, which he claimed would 'completely ruin' his life.

'People were playing pranks all day, and when the teacher came out of the doors I was being egged on by mates. It was a rush of blood to the head,' Mr Dowdle said. 'I regret what I did. I sent a letter of apology – but I've been told she never wants to hear from me again.'

Tim Gartside, the headmaster, said he would stand by his decision to exclude Mr Dowdle and described the prank as a 'planned assault'.

'Like many schools, we like to mark the end of Year 13 and students have enjoyed clever, tasteful and original pranks that have neither harmed nor humiliated,' Mr Gartside said. 'Jacob Dowdle's behaviour was not a prank. The school will always take a firm stance with students who assault staff in any way.'

(Katie Gibbons, *The Times*, May 2014)

Choose **four** statements below that are TRUE.

- Shade the boxes of the ones you think are true
- Choose a maximum of four statements.

A Jacob Dowdle immediately regretted what he had done.
B The teacher received Jacob's letter but said she did not wish to reply.
C Jacob Dowdle thinks the school's actions could wreck the rest of his life.
D The school's actions will have a long-term effect on Jacob Dowdle's career prospects.
E What Jacob Dowdle did was worse than what anyone else did.
F The headmaster will not change his decision to expel Jacob Dowdle.
G The school teaches its students how to carry out clever and original pranks.
H Although Jacob Dowdle used whipped cream, Mr Gartside did not find his actions tasteful.

Q2: Dealing with two texts and summarising

Paper 2, Question 2 will ask you to deal with both the non-fiction sources. You will have to write a **summary** of **some feature of both sources** – perhaps the differences between the situations or the characters in them.
There are 8 marks for this question so you will need to complete it in 8 or 9 minutes.

What, exactly, must I do?

You will have to identify the relevant points in each source, then link comparable ideas effectively. You should support what you say with appropriate quotations from the sources.

Text A

This is a speech made by a black woman in 1851.

> I think that 'twixt the negroes of the South and the women at the North, all talking about rights, the white men will be in a fix pretty soon. But what's all this here talking about?
>
> That man over there says that women need to be helped into carriages, and lifted over ditches, and to have the best place everywhere. Nobody ever helps me into carriages, or over mud-puddles, or gives me any best place! And ain't I a woman? Look at me! Look at my arm! I have ploughed and planted, and gathered into barns, and no man could head me! And ain't I a woman? I could work as much and eat as much as a man – when I could get it – and bear the lash as well! And ain't I a woman? I have borne thirteen children, and seen most all sold off to slavery, and when I cried out with my mother's grief, none but Jesus heard me! And ain't I a woman?
>
> That little man in black there, he says women can't have as much rights as men, 'cause Christ wasn't a woman! Where did your Christ come from? Where did your Christ come from? From God and a woman! Man had nothing to do with Him.
>
> If the first woman God ever made was strong enough to turn the world upside down all alone, these women together ought to be able to turn it back, and get it right side up again! And now they is asking to do it, the men better let them.

(Old Sojourner Woman's Convention in Ohio)

1 What is this woman saying about women's lives in 1851? List your ideas.

- ....
- ....
- ....
- ....
- ....

Workbook answers can be found at www.hoddereducation.co.uk/myrevisionnotes/gcse-english-language

- ....
- ....
- ....
....

Text B

This is from a modern newspaper column.

Every woman I know has been shouted at by a stranger. Every woman I know has been warned about walking back in the dark, even though they know that most acts of violence happen at home, by somebody they know. Every woman I know texts their friends to say they're home safe. Every woman I know in London has been warned about the temporary alleys around the back of Tottenham Court Road, where there are blindspots on CCTV. Every woman I know who appears on TV has been mocked for her appearance, for her desirability. Every female writer I know has been compared to a Nazi.

And every woman I know who has encountered this intimidation – in emails, tweets, below-the-line comments or after seeing intimate photographs shared by an ex – has been advised to laugh it off. To ignore it. But few of us do, and few of us can, because it's as much a part of the world we live in as the knowledge that we are in danger if we go out in shoes we can't run away in.

(Eva Wiseman, *The Observer Magazine*, 2014)

2 What sorts of problems are encountered by modern women? List your ideas.

- ....
- ....
- ....
- ....
- ....
- ....
- ....

AQA GCSE English Language Workbook

3 Complete this table, to make links between the points of view in Text A and Text B. Add brief quotations to support your notes.

	Text A	Text B
Positive or negative about the situation of women?		
What their lives are like		
How women are treated by men		
How women are expected to respond		
How women actually react		

4 Remembering to use your own words – apart from when you are quoting – summarise the differences in the lives of these two women.

Answer on lined paper.

Text A

This is part of a modern commentary on the execution of Joan of Arc. She led the French forces against the English in the Hundred Years' War, but was captured and burned to death in 1431.

The scene of her execution is vividly described by a number of those who were present that day. She listened calmly to the sermon read to her, but then broke down weeping during her own speech, in which she forgave her accusers for what they were doing and asked them to pray for her. The accounts say that most of the judges and assessors themselves, and a few of the English soldiers and officials, were openly sobbing by the end of it. But a few of the English soldiers were becoming impatient, and one sarcastically shouted to the bailiff Jean Massieu, 'What, priest, are you going to make us wait here until dinner?' The executioner was ordered to 'do your duty'.

They tied her to a tall pillar well above the crowd. She asked for a cross, which one sympathetic English soldier tried to provide by making a small one out of wood. A crucifix was brought from the nearby church and Friar Martin Ladvenu held it up in front of her until the flames rose. Several eyewitnesses recalled that she repeatedly screamed '…in a loud voice the holy name of Jesus, and implored and invoked without ceasing the aid of the saints of Paradise'. Then her head drooped, and it was over.

(Allen Williamson, http://archive.joan-of-arc.org)

5 Make notes on what we learn about:
- Joan

....

....

....

....

....

- the English

....

....

....

....

....

- what happened at her execution.

....

....

....

....

Text B

This is a description of the execution of Joan of Arc from a book written in the nineteenth century.

Judgement was finally entered up against the ill-used maid, who, on the 30th May, 1431, was brought in a cart to the market-place and burned at Rouen.

We would gladly draw a veil over the fate of poor Joan; but we are unwilling to spare those who were accessory to it, from the shame which increases whenever the facts are repeated. Cardinal Beaufort and some of the bishops who had been instrumental to the murder of the Maid began to whimper when the ceremony commenced, and to find it more than their natures could bear to witness. They had ordered the atrocity that was about to take place; but conscience had made them such cowards that they had not the courage to watch the carrying out of their own savage suggestions.

(Beckett and Abbott, *The Comic History of England*)

6 What does this report focus on?

....

....

....

7 How does the writer describe those who were responsible for the execution?

....

....

....

....

....

8 Make a list of the similarities and differences you can find in the two reports of Joan of Arc's death.

- Similarities:

....

....

....

....

....

Paper 2, Q2: Dealing with two texts and summarising

- Differences:

....
....
....
....
....
....

Extended practice

Write a summary of the differences in the two reports of Joan of Arc's death. Remember to use:

- your own words to explain the differences
- quotations to support what you say.

....
....
....
....
....
....
....
....
....
....
....
....
....
....
....
....

Continue on lined paper if necessary.

Q3: Analysing persuasive language

> Paper 2, Question 3 will ask you **how language** has been used to **influence opinion** in one of the non-fiction sources. You will have to identify the relevant language and to say what effect it is intended to have. You must use appropriate terminology ('simile', 'complex sentence', etc.). There are 12 marks for this question so you will need to complete it in 12 or 13 minutes.

> **What, exactly, must I do?**
> It is not enough simply to quote relevant sections of text and say that they are there 'to make you think' or 'to influence the reader'. Ideally, you need to be able to write about words and phrases, language features and techniques, and sentence forms – and to say how they work: what they suggest and what they make you think.

The family in this extract was driven from its home in China when the Communists took over. Much poorer, they then had to live in Malaya.

> Our house had no electricity or running water. Mosquitoes stung us on face and arms; sores from infected bites scarred our legs. In the house, ants crawled around cups or carried dead upturned cockroaches or beetles away like pallbearers. Lizards darted after insects on walls, their tails sometimes dropping on to the table and into the cups. My mother taught her children to read and told them stories by the light of a kerosene lamp. She looked elegant still, but the hands that held the book were roughened. A daughter died, then a son, and all because the hospitals were inadequate.
>
> (Lynn Pan, 'A Decision')

1 What impression of the writer's life do we get from the following quotations, and how is the language used to create the impression?

- 'stung … sores … scarred'

....

....

- 'ants crawled around cups'

....

....

- 'carried dead upturned cockroaches or beetles away like pallbearers'

....

....

Workbook answers can be found at www.hoddereducation.co.uk/myrevisionnotes/gcse-english-language

Paper 2, Q3: Analysing persuasive language

- 'ants crawled... lizards darted'

....

....

- 'the hands ... were roughened'

....

....

Consider how language is being used to persuade in this extract.

I really do mind the gap.

Imagine that you're selling something on eBay. Let's say it's an old sofa. The winning bidder seals the deal at £100. Only, when he comes to pick it up, he tells you it's going to have to be £80, because he's just noticed you're a woman. You'd tell him to get lost, right? We all would. So why do we treat the employers who purchase our services differently? Why are we so complacent about the 20% pay gap between men and women?

Some people deny there's a problem, or mis-categorise it as a 'women's issue'. The pay gap is invisible to The Men Who Run Things because they don't experience it…

(Lauren Laverne, *The Observer Magazine*, August 2014)

2 What is the style of the writing here?

....

....

....

....

....

3 How are the sentences being used? Write about the effect of:

- the opening three sentences

....

....

....

....

....

- the complex sentence that follows them

....

....

....

....

- the rhetorical sentences.

....

....

....

....

....

....

4 Comment on the sarcasm in the final paragraph.

....

....

....

....

This is an extract from an American newspaper in 1898.

Four Danbury men discovered a gigantic wild man last week in Cotton Hollow, a section of country between High Rock Grove and Naugatuck. They were Jerry Wilson, Howard Bradley, James Durbin and George Howes, and were working in that vicinity. On the night of their discovery, they had been spending the evening with friends near High Rock Grove and were returning through the woods to where they were staying, between 11 and 12 o'clock at night.

As they were trudging along, a man of gigantic stature sprang up in front of them from among the bushes and shouted out to Wilson, who was ahead:

'How far is it to the next town?'

'Three miles,' said Wilson, with his hair standing on end and his eyes almost bulging out of their sockets.

Without saying anything more, the giant started off on a wild run and disappeared in the woods and the dark. All four of the men had seen him, however, before he was out of sight, and they were satisfied that he was at least twice as tall as anyone of their party, and correspondingly as large every other way. They acknowledged to having been pretty thoroughly scared by his sudden appearance.

The next morning they commenced systematic investigations. They went back to the place and measured the foot tracks of the giant. They were 18½ inches long and 5½ inches broad. The heel alone measured 5 inches.

Paper 2, Q3: Analysing persuasive language

Then they made enquiries of the people who live in Cotton Hollow and were informed that such a man had been seen several times. He was known to be at least nine feet tall and to weigh not less than 500 pounds.

Unless the vision of these men was greatly magnified on that night, and unless the people of the neighbourhood told them a story to suit the occasion, they saw a character that a freak show could exhibit to the Englishmen as a specimen of American products. They are willing to swear to the truth of their statements, and are sure that they saw a man who would be a giant among giants.

(*Naugatuck Daily News*, June 1898)

5 How is language used to try to make the reader believe that this was a newsworthy event? Write about:

- how the scene is established in the opening paragraph

....
....
....
....
....

- the contrast between 'trudging' and 'sprang'

....
....
....
....

- 'with his hair standing on end and his eyes almost bulging out of their sockets'

....
....
....
....

- 'the giant started off on a wild run and disappeared in the woods and the dark'

....
....
....
....

- 'however', 'acknowledged', 'systematic investigations'

....

....

....

- the measurements

....

....

....

- the sentences and the language used in the final paragraph.

....

....

....

....

This is part of a speech made by Mahatma Gandhi in 1942. He was fighting peacefully for India's independence from the British. He wanted his country's freedom immediately, despite the fact that this was in the middle of World War II.

Although this speech was made to his own people, his intention was to persuade the British through what he said.

> Then, there is the question of your attitude towards the British. I have noticed that there is hatred towards the British among the people. The people say they are disgusted with their behaviour. The people make no distinction between British imperialism* and the British people. To them, the two are one. This hatred would even make them welcome the Japanese. It is most dangerous. It means that they will exchange one slavery for another. We must get rid of this feeling. Our quarrel is not with the British people, we fight their imperialism. The proposal for the withdrawal of British power did not come out of anger. It came to enable India to play its due part at the present critical juncture. It is not a happy position for a big country like India to be merely helping with money and material obtained willy-nilly from her while the United Nations are conducting the war. We cannot evoke the true spirit of sacrifice and valour, so long as we are not free. I know the British Government will not be able to withhold freedom from us, when we have made enough self-sacrifice. We must, therefore, purge ourselves of hatred. Speaking for myself, I can say that I have never felt any hatred. As a matter of fact, I feel myself to be a greater friend of the British now than ever before. One reason is that they are today in distress. My very friendship, therefore, demands that I should try to save them from their mistakes. As I view the situation, they are on the brink of an abyss. It, therefore, becomes my duty to warn them of their danger even though it may, for the time being, anger them to the point of cutting off the friendly hand that is stretched out to help them. People may laugh, nevertheless that is my claim. At a time when I may have to launch the biggest struggle of my life, I may not harbour hatred against anybody.
>
> (Mahatma Gandhi, 1942)

* Imperialism is the desire to rule over other countries.

Extended practice

How does Gandhi use language to influence the British to accept his views? Write about his views and the techniques he uses.

Continue on lined paper.

Q4: Comparing viewpoints and writers' methods

> Paper 2, Question 4 requires you to refer to the whole of **both** non-fiction sources and to **compare the writers' attitudes** to some given feature, such as, perhaps, their attitude to schools or to foreign travel. You will also have to **compare the methods** they use to present their ideas, such as humour, contrast, rhetoric, imagery. You must use appropriate quotations to support what you say. There are 16 marks for this question so you will need to complete it in 16 or 17 minutes.

> **What, exactly, must I do?**
> You need to show a detailed understanding of the similarities and/or differences between the ideas in the sources and to analyse how the writers have presented them. You will, therefore, be presenting two sets of comparisons – of the writers' attitudes and their methods – in the same answer.

Text A

This passage is from the 1840s.

> The little girl had entirely lost all childish ways. Her little face, pale and thin with privation, was wrinkled where the dimples ought to have been, and she would sigh frequently. When some hot dinner was offered to her, she would not touch it, because, if she ate too much 'it made her sick', she said, 'and she wasn't used to meat, only on a Sunday.'

> The poor child, although the weather was severe, was wrapped in a thin cotton gown, with a threadbare shawl wrapped round her shoulders. She wore no covering to her head, and the long rusty hair stuck out in all directions. When she walked, she shuffled along, for fear that the large carpet slippers that served her for shoes should slip off her feet.

> 'I am just eight years old. On and off, I've been very near a twelvemonth in the streets. My mother learned me to needlework and to knit when I was about five. I used to go to school, too; but I wasn't there long. The master used to whack me. He hit me three times, ever so hard, across the face with the cane. That's why I left school.'

(Henry Mayhew, 'London')

1. What does the writer make you think about this girl and her situation? (What is his attitude to her?)
   List as many points as you can, with quotations to support them.

- ....
- ....
- ....
- ....
- ....
- ....
- ....

2 What methods does the writer use to present the girl to the reader? List points about each paragraph in turn.

Paragraph 1. Consider:
- the opening sentence
- the verbs and adjectives
- the final sentence.

....

....

....

....

....

....

....

Paragraph 2. Consider:
- how the detail is presented in the first sentence
- 'long rusty hair stuck out in all directions'
- how the final sentence affects the reader.

....

....

....

....

....

....

Paragraph 3. Consider:
- how the girl speaks
- the details
- the sentences.

....

....

....

....

....

AQA GCSE English Language Workbook

Text B

This text is taken from the diary of an English nurse who helped care for refugees in Russia during World War I. Here, she tells of people who had been forced to flee from their homes and were living together in a huge shed. She is taking presents to them at Christmas.

In the lower part of the barak especially there were some very dark corners, and the children who lived in them looked greenly pale and sickly, like potato-sprouts that have been kept too long in a cellar. And outside the barak was a world of light and freedom – a world where the sun was shining and the air cold and invigorating.

'Don't these children ever go out?' I asked of one of the mothers.

'No, it is too cold; we have no outdoor clothes and no boots and stockings for them. We left our village in the summer and have only our summer clothes here,' she replied.

I looked round and it was true. The children were in their cotton dresses and suits, and many of them were barefoot, and I remembered then seeing two little boys just outside the barak who were running barefoot in the snow, despite the state of their little red toes, raw and bleeding from the cold.

'But they have been here three or four months now. Don't the children even go to school?'

'No, the schools can't take them. They are afraid. We have measles and scarlet fever here in the barak. Sometimes three or four children die here in one day. I myself have lost two. But what is to be done? Others suffer still more.'

Words are little use when one is face to face with the bare facts of life.

We got one of the biggest boys, a lad of about sixteen, to arrange the children in single file all along one side of the table where the presents were set out, and to make a passage through the crowd so they could return the other way. They were very docile, and good, poor little souls, and quickly understood what was expected of them. One by one they shyly advanced, received their bag, and scuttered away exactly like shy, friendly little robins who overcome their timidity in a hard winter and venture near for food.

(Violetta Thurston, *The People Who Run: Being the tragedy of the refugees in Russia*)

3 How does the writer feel about these children? (What is her attitude to them?)
Make as many points as you can, with quotations to support them.

Paper 2, Q4: Comparing viewpoints and writers' methods

4 What methods does the writer use to present her ideas?
Complete this table.

Method	Quotation	Explanation of effect(s)
Opens with simile	'like potato-sprouts that have been kept too long in the cellar'	Links to emotive adjectives ('greenly pale and sickly') Just 'sprouts' (not growing properly) 'sprouts' suggests they could grow, if only they were in the right environment 'cellar' illustrates the unnatural world of the barak
....	....	....
....	....	....
....	....	....
....	....	....
....	....	....
....	....	....

49

AQA GCSE English Language Workbook

5 Re-read both of the texts in this unit.

Compare how the two writers convey their attitudes to the children they are describing.

In your answer:
- Compare the writers' attitudes.
- Compare the methods they use to convey their attitudes.
- Support your ideas with quotations from both texts.

....

Continue on lined paper if necessary.

Text A

This passage is from a letter written by a soldier in Wellington's army fighting against Napoleon. The soldiers at that time were often beaten by the officers.

Lord C — drew up a long string of charges against Major Hudson, who had the choice to be court martialled or retire from the army. The Major chose the latter.

Thus the regiment is ridded of as great a tyrant as ever disgraced the army. This man delighted in torturing the men; every soldier hated him. When once a soldier came under his lash, it was no use for any officer to plead for him. If he was young, his reply was: 'It will do him good, make him know better for the future.' On the other hand, if he was getting into years, the brute would say, 'Oh! He is old enough to know better.' He delighted in going round the barracks on a Sunday morning to see if he could catch any of the married people roasting their meat. If he saw any meat roasting, he would cut it down, and carry away the string and nail in his pocket, observing that they should boil their meat, it was more nourishing. Once he paid a visit to the hospital and saw a cat. 'Whose cat is this,' said he. 'It is mine, Sir,' said the Hospital Sergeant's wife. 'We are very much troubled with rats and mice.' 'I don't care a damn,' was the reply, 'you know my order, I will neither have dogs, cats, rats or mice here.'

His departure caused quite a celebration amongst the Regiment.

(B.H. Liddell Hart, *The Letters of Private Wheeler, 1809–1828*)

6 What is the writer's attitude to Major Hudson? Explain.
Make just detailed notes. Support your ideas with quotations.

7 List the methods the writer uses to convey his ideas, supporting what you say with evidence.

Text B

This is from a letter written by a captain in the First World War who has just been demoted.

I suppose you have learned that I am at present under a cloud. I have been kicked out of my command of 'D' Company. The strained relations between myself and Colonel Stewart had to come to a head, and as I was under his command, I had to be the one to go. It is the way of the Army. I am not the sort of man he likes, and the only reassuring thing that I can say about it is that I am glad I am not that sort of man.

He is a pig. (It is against the Censorship Regulations to say so in a letter, and yet I mean no insult to the pig.) He does not like me, and I very emphatically dislike him. But in the matter of personal likes and dislikes in the Army the senior officer always has the advantage.

I wanted to appeal to the General. The real general unfortunately had just gone down sick, and his place was being occupied by a Brigadier who was a school companion of Colonel Stewart. They call each other by their Christian names. This acting Commander said that Col. Stewart's judgement was enough for him. I offered to get a report on my efficiency from my previous Commanding Officer. But it was no use.

And so I am under a cloud. Just for the moment I am in the Army but not of it. I have no work to do. I am not enjoying the war a bit. When German aeroplanes drop bombs back here the whole night through, I do not shout: 'To arms! To arms! The foe!', I merely feel very much annoyed, and think hard thoughts of the Devil, the German State, and my Commanding Officer each in turn, until I fall asleep. You see what a dangerous rebel I am…

(Letter from Willie Ferrie, May 1918)

8 What is this writer's attitude towards the officers?
Make notes that explain your views. Support your ideas with quotations.

Paper 2, Q4: Comparing viewpoints and writers' methods

9 List the methods the writer uses to convey his ideas.

....

....

....

....

....

....

....

....

....

....

....

....

....

10 Make notes to compare the attitudes to the officers and methods used to present them in Text A and Text B.

	Text A	Text B
attitudes to officers		
methods used		

53

Extended practice

Re-read the texts on pages 51 and 52.

Compare how the soldiers in Texts A and B convey their different attitudes to officers. In your answer, you should:

- Compare their attitudes.
- Compare the methods they use to convey those attitudes.
- Support your ideas with quotations from both texts.

Continue on lined paper if necessary.

About the Section B questions

In Section B of Paper 1 you will be offered a choice of two essay questions, in which you will have to write to **describe** or to **narrate** (tell a story). In Paper 2 there will be just one question, asking you to give your **point of view** on a given topic.

What, exactly, must I do?

On both papers, you should spend approximately 60 minutes on Section A. This will leave you 45 minutes for Section B. You will have to produce just one response for Section B on each paper.

Paper 1

Paper 1 will give you a choice of two questions and you must choose just **one** of them. You will be presented with one of the following alternatives:

- two questions asking you to describe
- two questions asking you to produce a piece of narrative writing (a story)
- one question asking you to produce a piece of description and one asking you to write a narrative.

It is unwise to try to answer both questions, because this means both responses tend to be rushed and often underdeveloped. Although your best mark will count towards your total, the marks for both are likely to be disappointing.

Instead, decide which question you can handle best and try to respond carefully and in detail.

Paper 2

You will have no choice on Paper 2. One question will be offered, which you will have to answer.

The question will ask for your point of view on some issue. You will be told the topic, the audience for which you are writing (for example, the Prime Minister, or the readers of a national newspaper), and the form of writing you have to produce (perhaps a speech, or an article, or a letter).

How to divide up your time

If you are wise, you will spend:

- four or five minutes planning
- thirty-five minutes writing
- five minutes checking and improving your work.

It is worth remembering that the best responses are almost always planned in advance and checked carefully at the end.

The marks will be awarded in the same way for both papers:

24 marks	For content and organisation	Ideas, ability to target purpose and audience, structure, paragraphing and use of language.
16 marks	For technical accuracy	Sentences, punctuation, spelling, vocabulary and use of Standard English.

Importantly, do not think that the more you write, the higher will be your mark. Examiners are looking for quality, not quantity. It is far better to produce two-and-a-half pages of interesting and accurate writing than to write five pages that are unstructured and full of repetition and errors.

Communicating effectively

Part of your Section B mark is awarded for how effectively you communicate: how well your writing targets the required **purpose and audience**. This means you must write appropriately, using the appropriate **tone**, **style** and **register**, and channelling your ideas so you respond to the **question that has been asked**.

What, exactly, must I do?

To ensure your writing is effective and hits the required purpose and audience, read the question carefully and underline the important words if that helps you focus on the task. Plan in detail (see Organising your writing, page 58) and follow that plan. As you write, glance back occasionally at the title, to make sure you are still 'on track'. Throughout, use the appropriate tone, style and register. This means you must write in Standard English and remember for whom you are writing: on Paper 1, you are writing for the examiner; on Paper 2, make sure you are writing the correct kind of text (letter, article, speech…) and for the given audience (your Member of Parliament, broadsheet newspaper readers, parents…).

In response to the task 'Describe the place you love the most', a Grade 3 student wrote:

    It's not the best place in the world but I'm dead fond of the Lake
    District but that might be cos I'm dragged there every year by my mum
    and dad who do love the place so I'm, like, oh, not again, but when we
    get there I always think it could be worse and I enjoy a lot of stuff
    going on.

1 Write an improved version of this extract with a better tone and style.

....

....

....

....

....

Task: Write a short story that begins, 'I never knew what Stevie was going to do next.' This is a Grade 3 opening:

    It was crazy in the house. Everybody were dancing and singing and the
    lads from down the road had brought booze, which was gonna make Dannie's
    parents go ape when they got back from the do at the local dive they
    called their local.

2 Write an improved version that targets the title much more precisely and is more likely to impress the examiner.

....

....

....

This is a Grade 3 opening to a response produced when a student was asked to 'Write a speech, to be given to a meeting of local headteachers, to give your views on how careers education should be delivered in schools.'

```
Let's face it guys, as it stands careers ed is useless, innit? We don't learn
nothing any time and it doesn't get us fit to do anything at all when we get
out of this prison and start to have life at last. I mean, sort it!
```

3 Improve this opening so it is appropriate for the audience.

Extended practice

Remembering to use Standard English, write an opening paragraph for one of the following tasks:

- Describe the scene in a local park.
- Write a story entitled 'The End of the Line'.
- Write an article for your school website, in which you give your views on the quality of your school's facilities (you might wish to comment on sports facilities, classrooms, dining areas, etc.).

Organising your writing

Part of your Section B mark is for organisation: how well you **structure** your response. This means that the ideas must be in a logical order, so that they **develop effectively** from the opening to the ending. When you are writing, ideas also need to be **linked well**, for which you need to use connectives appropriately.

What, exactly, must I do?

It is best to have a planning system, so that you know precisely what you are going to write before you begin: the more detailed it is, the better. Consider a four-stage process:

1 Underline the most significant words in the title.
2 Produce a rapid spider diagram with four or five main ideas.
3 Turn the ideas into an ordered list, which might well represent your paragraphs.
4 Beneath each sub-heading, add other ideas and features that you intend to include in that section of your response.

As you write the actual response, make sure the ideas are connected. Read everything through – 'out loud' in your head – and be prepared to improve the expression. Remember that there are no marks for neatness.

1 You are going to produce a detailed plan for this task: <u>Describe</u> an <u>unforgettable</u> event.
   - Produce a spider diagram of ideas.

- Convert the ideas into a logical sequence. Add 'Opening' as another idea, at the top, and 'Ending' at the bottom. Leave two or three lines under each of the sub-headings you have now created. Decide where you might include a short paragraph for effect.

....

....

....

....

....

....

....

....

....

....

....

....

....

....

....

....

....

....

....

- Add jotted details under each heading, to suggest what will go in that section. These might include: vocabulary, examples, quotations, specific details, similes and rhetorical phrases you might use; where you might add conversation, short sentences or an ellipsis; lists…

2 To practise using different openings:

- Begin your response with a brief conversation.

....

....

....

....

- Begin with a description of the scene, or of your emotions.

3 To practise finishing your response, produce the endings suggested below. Make sure each links back to one of your openings.

- End with a summary of how you felt afterwards.

- End in a totally different way.

Extended practice

1 Produce a full, detailed plan for the title below.
  Title: Someone once said, 'We all need some adventure in our lives.'
         Give your views on this statement.
2 Write an opening and an ending for this title, which are suitably linked in some way.

<u>Spider diagram</u>

<u>Detailed list of content</u>

Continue on lined paper and write your opening and ending on lined paper too.

Vocabulary and crafting

> Part of your Section B mark is for your vocabulary: that is, the **quality** and **appropriateness** of the language you use. You will be using **Standard English** throughout, and you should aim for vocabulary that will **impress** the examiner. So, for example, you will probably be focusing on vivid adjectives, varied verbs and possibly imagery when describing; narrative connectors when narrating (and probably, in this case, touches of realistic – possibly colloquial – speech); and the full range of linguistic techniques to argue and persuade when offering your viewpoint.

> **What, exactly, must I do?**
> Always remember, when you are writing, that the examiner wants to see varied, high-quality vocabulary, accurately used. Never 'dumb down' unless you are quoting someone briefly; always use the 'best words' you know – even if you are not absolutely certain you can spell them correctly. You will be rewarded for your ambition even if you make a spelling error.

1 Add some interesting adjectives, verbs and adverbs to this description.

The man was .... (adjective). He did not really walk into the surgery – instead, he seemed to .... (verb) .... (adverb), as if each step was a struggle.

When he had registered, he .... (verb) on to a .... (adjective) chair, his chest .... (verb). .... (adverb), he pulled himself together. He .... (verb) down at his feet, looking surprised that he had made it.

2 Fill in the gaps in this extract with high-quality vocabulary.

The mountain .... To our left, the range of hills .... like .... The sun was .... and it felt as if .... We were as .... as .... , with the whole day stretching ahead, ...

3 Write a very short description of an assembly. Try to include:
   - interesting verbs, adjectives and adverbs
   - at least one simile or metaphor.

....

....

....

....

Vocabulary and crafting

4 Decide what better words or phrases you might use to replace the ones indicated here, in this section from a narrative.

After the fight, he (went) .... down the road with (a smile on his face)

....

He felt (wonderful) ....

The sun shone (brightly) ....; he (walked with confidence) ....;

and he was sure (things would pick up now) ....

5 Improve this opening to a short story by adding effective links, better vocabulary generally and perhaps a touch of conversation.

```
She sat and looked at the sea. It was grey. Now that she had run away,
she did not know what to do. A boy sat down next to her. He was about
sixteen. She decided to talk to him and ask him if there was anyone in
this place who could help her. She was frightened though. But he seemed
friendly.
```

....

....

....

....

....

....

....

6 Write the opening lines to a short story entitled 'The Feast'.
Grab the examiner's attention with your vocabulary.

....

....

....

....

7 Improve the vocabulary in this extract, which offers a view on family life.
Include:
- more impressive words and phrases
- connectives
- rhetoric to persuade the reader.

> I can't wait to leave home. My mum and dad drive me mad and they think everything that happens is my fault. I feel like shutting them up for good. As soon as I'm sixteen, I'm out that door for good and they won't see me for dust. Then, they can find some other sucker to do the washing up, because it won't be me. Not a chance.

....

....

....

....

....

....

....

Extended practice

Write a section of your response to this task: Write a speech to be given to a headteachers' conference, to give your views on whether children should always have to attend the school nearest to their house.

Use vocabulary that will impress your audience. Possibly:

- rhetorical questions
- quotations
- repetition for effect
- anecdote or examples.

....

....

....

....

....

....

....

....

Vocabulary and crafting

Using effective punctuation

> You will be assessed on the **quality** and **range** of your punctuation in each of your Section B responses. This will make up part of your mark for **accuracy**.

> **What, exactly, must I do?**
> Ideally, you should be trying to use the full range of punctuation – and using it accurately. If you can also demonstrate the ability to use punctuation with some imagination (for example, blending dashes, speech marks and perhaps an ellipsis within the same sentence), that will impress the examiner still further.

1 Add all the necessary full stops, capital letters and commas in this extract.

When we arrived at the house no one was there that was when it got scary and we decided to head off into the woods which afterwards seemed a silly thing to do at the time though we just thought it was for the best and angie led us away.

2 Use apostrophes to abbreviate these phrases.

	Abbreviation
He would not	He wouldn't
I cannot run	
That is crazy	
I am not mad – you are	

3 Write a short paragraph giving your views on pollution.
Use three rhetorical questions and an exclamation – and the correct punctuation.

....

....

....

....

....

4 Write a paragraph to follow the one you have just written on pollution. This time, include:
- brackets
- at least one dash
- an ellipsis.

....

....

Workbook answers can be found at www.hoddereducation.co.uk/myrevisionnotes/gcse-english-language

Using effective punctuation

....

....

....

5 Punctuate this dialogue.

Hello said the woman to the little girl next door
The little girl looked at her with tears in her eyes and replied hiya
Why said the woman are you digging that hole
I have to said the girl
But why
My hamster is dead said the little girl there is going to be a burial
Oh im sorry but why is the hole so big asked the woman
The little girl looked at her with an evil glint in her eye. It has to be quite big she said my hamster is inside your cat

6 Add colons and semi-colons to this paragraph.

The town was sleeping the pavements were deserted, with only the litter shifting in the breeze hardly a car moved on the roads and the birdsong could be heard clearly from the tops of the trees. A homeless man struggled to his feet in a shop doorway the police would be carrying out their routine sweep soon.

Extended practice

Write a description of a town centre on a Saturday afternoon.
Try to include all the punctuation marks you have practised in this unit.

....

....

....

....

....

....

....

....

....

Continue on lined paper.

Improving sentences and grammar

> The examiner will assess you on the **range and effectiveness of the sentences and grammar** in each of your Section B responses. This will make up part of your mark for accuracy.

> **What, exactly, must I do?**
>
> You need to begin and end your sentences clearly, though that is really a matter of punctuation.
>
> You should also use simple, compound and complex sentences and, if possible, try to use sentences for effect – perhaps using one or two short sentences to suggest surprise, or long sentences to present complex descriptions; or using a rhetorical sentence, or minor sentences to present a series of emotions…

1 Use three simple sentences to show the emotions of someone who has just been embarrassed in public. (A simple sentence has just one clause.)

....

....

2 Write two compound sentences to describe a busy marketplace, market hall or mall. (Compound sentences are made up of simple sentences linked by 'and', 'but' etc.)

....

....

....

3 Write a complex sentence that presents the thoughts of a woman who is about to resign from her job. (A complex sentence includes clauses that would not make sense on their own.)

....

....

....

4 Write a paragraph that gives your views on whether or not sex education should begin in primary schools. Include a variety of sentences.

....

....

....

68 Workbook answers can be found at www.hoddereducation.co.uk/myrevisionnotes/gcse-english-language

Improving sentences and grammar

5 Write a short paragraph in which a terrified person tries to escape from a country's secret police. Use a long sentence as they flee, then short sentences to present a climax.

....

....

....

....

....

6 Write a short paragraph that opens with one-word sentences to show how the person, now facing execution, feels. Then, use one long sentence, which itself builds to a climax.

....

....

....

....

....

7 Write a short paragraph that shows how the person's relatives react after the event. Include a rhetorical question, a list and a sentence that fades away with an ellipsis…

....

....

....

....

....

Extended practice

Write a short description of your favourite place in the world.
Use a variety of sentence types.

Use lined paper for your response.

Paper 1, Section B: Writing to describe

Section B of Paper 1 will offer you a choice of two tasks – you must complete just one of them. There will be two 'writing to describe' titles **or** two 'writing to narrate' titles **or** one of each (writing to narrate is covered on pages 80–89). One of the titles will always be supported with a picture. If you are writing to describe, you will probably be asked to describe **a place**, **a person** or **an event**. Marks will be awarded for the content, and for how well it is organised and for the technical accuracy of your work. You will have 45 minutes to produce your response.

What, exactly, must I do?

Select the task that is best for you and ensure you know exactly what is required. Spend about 5 minutes planning it. Then, in 35 minutes, you will probably write two or three sides: it is better to write two sides that are impressive than five sides that are not. At the end, take 5 minutes to check through your writing carefully and correct and improve it.

Describing a scene

Consider this task:
Write a description suggested by this picture.

1 To help describe the crowds, think of:

- three adjectives

....

- three similes

    1 ....

    2 ....

    3 ....

70 Workbook answers can be found at www.hoddereducation.co.uk/myrevisionnotes/gcse-english-language

- two metaphors.

    1 ....

    2 ....

2 Write three sentences or phrases to describe the setting.

    1 ....

    2 ....

    3 ....

3 Think of two sentences to describe the weather.

    1 ....

    2 ....

4 Using some of the ideas above, write two paragraphs describing the scene.

....

....

....

....

....

....

....

....

....

....

....

....

5 You are now going to write sections of a description of a traffic jam. Write:

- the opening: possibly consider beginning with a view from a police helicopter, or by using a strong image, or by describing the smell and noise…

....

....

- a paragraph in which people are talking: maybe people in a car, or people passing, or a discussion on a radio of the traffic jam...

- a paragraph that captures the frustrations of those trapped: consider using an extended metaphor and/or the thoughts of an individual...

- the ending: which links back to the start in some way and/or possibly brings the traffic jam to an end or implies it will go on much longer.

Paper 1, Section B: Writing to describe

Describing a person

You have been asked to describe a member of your family.

6 Jot down notes to complete this table.

Ideas for inclusion	Details
Their looks	
First memories of them	
Their past	
Their interests	
Their best qualities	
How they behave	
What they talk about/ how they talk	
Their failings	
Why they are loved/ disliked	

7 Write an opening paragraph for your description.
You could begin a description by putting this person in a situation and describing how they behave, before moving on to describe them more generally.

....

....

....

....

....

....

8 Write a brief anecdote that captures the person's personality.

....

....

....

....

....

....

9 Write a conversation that illustrates their personality.

....

....

....

....

....

....

10 Write six similes or metaphors that describe them or how they behave.

1 ....

2 ....

3 ....

Paper 1, Section B: Writing to describe

4 ....

5 ....

6 ....

11 Write a final paragraph that links back to your opening and adds some new thought(s) about this person.

....

....

....

....

....

....

Describe an event

Task: Describe a family party.

12 Briefly, decide why the party is being held: jot down the main details.

....

....

....

75

13 You cannot write in detail about everyone who attends; make notes on two or three individuals and identify important things about them.

....

....

....

....

....

....

14 Jot notes on what you need to say to describe the place where the party is being held.

....

....

....

....

15 Although your focus is on description, events will be taking place. List the ones you will include.

....

....

....

....

....

....

16 Produce a detailed plan for your description of a family party.

- Remember that you are writing to describe.
- Include all the important details and ensure you have an interesting opening and a memorable ending.

Spider diagram

Detailed list

17 Write the first page of your description of a family party.
Make sure you include:
- some imagery
- snatches of conversation
- use of the senses: taste, touch, hearing and smell, as well as what you can see
- description of the people and the place.

Extended practice

Write a description of bonfire night.

1 Plan

Bonfire night

2 Write your response on lined paper. Spend no more than 35 minutes on this part of the task. When you have 'finished', spend 5 minutes checking your work carefully.

Remember you will be assessed on:

- ideas and structure
- technical accuracy.

Paper 1, Section B: Writing to narrate

Section B of Paper 1 will offer you a choice of two tasks – you must complete just one of them. There will be two 'writing to describe' titles **or** two 'writing to narrate' titles **or** one of each (writing to describe was covered on pages 70–79). One of the titles will always be supported with a picture. If you are writing to narrate, you will probably be asked to write **a short story**, but you could be asked to write **a section of a longer story** – perhaps the opening of a novel. Marks will be awarded for the content and how well it is organised and for the technical accuracy of your work. You will have 45 minutes to produce your response.

What, exactly, must I do?

Select the task that is best for you and focus on exactly what is required. So, for example, if you are told to write a story that ends 'The torment was over', it is important to end your story with that line. Remember, too, not to try to achieve too much. You have a limited amount of time, so keep the core of your story short – perhaps just two or three scenes, with just two or three main characters.

Spend about 5 minutes planning it. Then, in 35 minutes, you will probably write two or three sides: it is better to write two sides that are impressive than five sides that are not. At the end, take 5 minutes to check through your writing carefully and to correct and improve it.

1 Decide on a narrative you could use in response to this task:
Write a short story entitled 'They were made for each other'.

Remember that stories usually:

- establish a situation
- have a trigger that sparks off the main events
- introduce challenge or conflict – which will be closely connected to the trigger
- then gradually become more exciting as they build to the climax or resolution.

Write a basic list of a possible train of events for this title.

....

....

....

....

....

....

....

Paper 1, Section B: Writing to narrate

This is a section from a Grade 4 response to the same title:

> He came in and she was upset. They had a huge row. Everyone was watching and then she stormed out and was crying in the garden. He just went back to his mates and chatted as if nothing had happened. Everybody just stared but he didn't care. Her friend went out to try to help her, but she didn't get far with that.

2 Take some part of this and develop it so it is more detailed and more interesting.

....

....

....

....

....

....

3 Write alternative openings to your story that will grab the reader's attention, using:

- a description of a setting

....

....

....

....

....

....

- the entry of a significant character

....

....

....

....

....

....

- dramatic action.

4 Write the trigger section.

5 Write the section that involves the climax.

Paper 1, Section B: Writing to narrate

Task: Write a story inspired by this picture.

6 Decide on your story.
   Jot down the sequence of events.

....

....

....

....

....

....

....

....

7 Begin to tell the story from different viewpoints, using:

- a first person narrator

....

....

....

....

....

AQA GCSE English Language Workbook

....

....

- an omniscient narrator, who knows everything

....

....

....

....

....

....

....

- a conversation, with the man or the woman talking to a friend or doctor

....

....

....

....

....

....

- a focus on a researcher, who is producing a programme on the loss of loved ones and how it can affect individuals

....

....

....

....

....

- a dramatic opening that is actually the ending of the narrative (i.e. after the opening, the story will go back in time to reveal what has happened and why).

8 Write four different endings for your story. You can finish what happens just as you planned earlier, but present the ending in different ways so that the endings match four of the openings you produced for Question 7.
So, for example, you could:
- use a first person or omniscient narrator
- return to the conversation one of the characters had
- return to the idea of the programme a researcher is producing
- link up with the dramatic opening.

Ending 1: ....

Ending 2: ....

Ending 3: ....

....

....

....

....

....

Ending 4: ....

....

....

....

....

....

Task: Write the opening section of a novel in which someone inherits great wealth.

In this case, your story will not conclude as it is only the opening section of a novel. Your response will introduce key characters and themes, and will end in an interesting way so the reader will want to read on.

9 Think of a basic idea for the novel.

....

....

....

....

10 Decide, simply, what will happen in your opening section.

....

....

....

....

11 Identify three characters you will introduce and jot notes briefly saying what each one is like.

1 ....

2 ....

3 ....

12 Jot down notes on the setting for your opening.

....

....

....

....

13 Decide what themes you will introduce in your opening (e.g. how parents treat their children, or how wealth can corrupt people).

1 ....

2 ....

3 ....

14 Write the opening of your response: try to include a hint of at least one of your themes.

....

....

....

....

....

....

....

15 Write the ending of your response.

....

....

....

....

Extended practice

Plan a story with the title 'Just like on TV'.

Write your story.

Continue on lined paper if necessary.

Paper 2, Section B: Writing with a viewpoint

Section B of Paper 2 will consist of just one task, which you must complete. You will be asked to give your **views** on a topic that is **connected to the texts in Section A**. You are likely to be asked to write an **article**, a **letter** or a **speech**; and your audience will also be made clear. Your **audience** might, for example, be the readers of a local newspaper or a gathering of international sports stars. Marks will be awarded for the content and how well it is organised and for the technical accuracy of your work. You will have 45 minutes to produce your response.

What, exactly, must I do?

You should identify exactly what the task requires – possibly by underlining the significant words – then plan your ideas in detail so that they develop logically. Try to include different features to add interest, such as examples, anecdotes, quotations and statistics. As you write your response, remember your audience and target them appropriately. Try to move effectively from a striking opening to an ending that is linked to it. Check your writing carefully when you have 'finished'.

Task: An article in a newspaper offered this opinion: 'You do not need to go abroad to have a good holiday.' Write a letter to the newspaper, giving your views on this idea.

1 What are the qualities and weaknesses of the following student opening?

```
You do not need to go abroad to have a good holiday because Britain
is great, isn't it? Else why would it be called Great Britain? It's
obvious. I went on holiday with my family to Fuerteventura and I hated
it because it was baking hot and dry and the wind was howling all the
time. You don't get that sort of thing in Devon. Well, you might get the
wind, but not the other stuff. And that is why holidays in Britain are
much better than anywhere else.
```

Qualities	Weaknesses

2 You must try to make your own response engaging.
Making up details that you might need, list:

- two quotations you could use in your letter to the newspaper

    1 ....

    2 ....

- three statistics to support your view

    1 ....

    2 ....

    3 ....

- details of an anecdote – a short story to prove a point – that you might include

    ....

    ....

    ....

- three similes you could use at some point – perhaps about the British weather, or the problems of air travel…

    1 ....

    2 ....

    3 ....

- three rhetorical questions to help persuade the reader to agree with your point of view.

    1 ....

    2 ....

    3 ....

3 Write down some persuasive connectives that would help your viewpoint to seem convincing.

It must be obvious to everyone…, Surely…, ...

....

AQA GCSE English Language Workbook

4 Set out your letter headings formally, including:

- your address
- the date
- the name and address of the person to whom you are writing
- 'Dear…'

....

5 Write an opening section for your response.
You might include:

- a rhetorical question
- some other feature to impress the examiner
- a range of sentences and punctuation.

Try *not* to:
- simply repeat the title to begin
- use a chatty approach.

Importantly, make sure you are writing in Standard English.

....

6 Write a detailed paragraph from the middle of your response, perhaps including some examples or an anecdote. Follow it with a short paragraph for effect.

....
....
....
....
....
....
....
....
....

7 Write three different endings for your letter. You could, for example, conclude with:

- some sarcasm
- a powerful list of three
- a quotation
- statistics...

You might also want to include a colon or semi-colon(s).
Although you are likely to be using different techniques from your opening, it will be most impressive if your ending links back to how you began, in some way.

Ending 1: ....
....
....
....
....
....

Ending 2: ....
....
....
....

Ending 3: ....

....

....

....

....

....

....

Task: Write an article for a broadsheet newspaper, in which you give your views on this statement: 'We are nearing the end of the world, because mankind will destroy itself.'

8 Often, simply generating ideas can be the hardest task.
  List five things about which you might choose to write; possibly the topics for your paragraphs.

  1 ....

  2 ....

  3 ....

  4 ....

  5 ....

9 Take one of those ideas and write a paragraph about it. Try to impress by using varied vocabulary and punctuation and by being clear about your viewpoint.

....

....

....

....

....

....

....

Paper 2, Section B: Writing with a viewpoint

You are likely to use rhetorical features in any response to Paper 2, Section B.

10 Look back at the paragraph you have just written in Question 9 and try to improve it by including:

- three rhetorical questions
- a one-word sentence for emphasis
- an appeal to the reader's common sense.

....

....

....

....

....

....

....

....

....

11 Write another paragraph. This time, set out your view supported by facts or statistics; then add a one-line or one-sentence paragraph to challenge the reader to disagree.

....

....

....

....

....

....

....

....

....

AQA GCSE English Language Workbook

12 Write a conclusion in which you:

- mock the opposite point of view
- use repetition to hammer home your points
- include sarcasm if you can.

....

....

....

....

....

....

....

....

Extended practice

Task: A conference for headteachers and government ministers for education has been discussing this opinion: 'It is simple: boys and girls should always be educated separately.'

You have been asked, as a student, to make a speech to the conference, offering your views on whether or not this system should be adopted in all schools in the country.

- Collect your initial ideas in a spider diagram.

- Transfer your ideas to a numbered list. After each sub-heading, note down details and features you will use in that section or paragraph.

....

....

....

....

....

....

....

....

....

....

....

....

- Write your response.

....

....

....

....

....

....

....

....

....

....

....

Continue on lined paper.

How to revise for the English Language exam

If you have worked through this book, and especially if you have also used *My Revision Notes*, you will be well prepared for the exam itself. It is sensible, however, to build on the practices you have already completed. You can revise thoroughly for English Language very easily – and almost always in neat, five-minute sessions! What could be more manageable?

The key is to focus on each question in turn and to remind yourself exactly what the examiner is looking for. That is not as difficult as it seems, because the exam papers are so predictable.

Once you've done this, organise a timetable depending on the time available, so that:

- If you are six months away from the exam, you spend 5 minutes each day on your English, working on a different skill each time.
- If it is three months to the Big Day, you spend two sessions of 5 minutes each day.
- If you are just a month away from the exam when you start revising, ideally you will be spending six lots of 5 minutes on your English Language each day – or as much as you can manage!

So, exactly how do I practise?

Pick and complete a task from the tables below each time, but pay particular attention to any of the skills with which you feel less confident.

Paper 1, Section A

Q1	Finding details	Read the opening page of a novel or the first paragraphs of a magazine story. **Find and underline details** that tell you about a character or the setting or what is happening.
Q2	Writing about language	Choose two paragraphs from a story and ask yourself: if I were in the exam, **which bits of language would I write about? What would I say about them?** Jot down notes if you wish – but the exercise can also be done in your head.
Q3	Dealing with structure	**Take a section of a story and decide how it has been put together.** What makes the opening interesting? How does it develop? Do we get an increasing knowledge of a character? Are there contrasts? Or surprises? Do the words link to create an ongoing impression? Are the sentences used for effect? Are the paragraphs used for effect?
Q4	Evaluating writers' methods	Choose an opening and **ask yourself: 'How good is it? Why?'** Look at how the writer has tried to interest you (with words, actions, techniques). At another time, ask yourself whether you are supposed to like a particular character, or to despise her, and why and how that impression has been created. Next time, ask yourself: what are the themes and how successfully are they put across? Or, how is the setting made clear and interesting?

Paper 2, Section A

Q1	Finding what is true	Work with a friend. Ask them to find four things in a newspaper article that are true (some might be things that are being suggested); ask them to write them down – and also to write four things that are close to being true, but aren't really. You then **decide which four things are true** and not just opinions or simply incorrect.
Q2	Dealing with two texts and summarising	It is hard to find two texts that can be compared, but you can **always practise summarising the main points in just** one text. In this case, just jot down some quick notes. If you can find two reports of the same thing – perhaps of a demonstration or a tragic accident – you can draw up a quick grid, and **put the comparable** features next to each other.
Q3	Analysing the effect of language	As with Paper 1, Question 2, find a short text and **decide which language you would write about in the exam and what you would say**. In this case, you will be using a non-fiction text: one from a newspaper will be fine.
Q4	Comparing two sources and writers' methods	As with Question 2, you can **practise the basic skill on just one source**. Ask yourself: what methods is the writer using to put across a message? If you have two articles or reports on the same subject, you can again draw up a quick practice grid and put **points of comparison** next to each other.

Section Bs

	Organising your writing	Make up a title and **spend 5 minutes producing a detailed plan** for it. On another occasion, write an **attention-grabbing opening** for the title. On another occasion, write an **impressive ending** for the title that links with the opening.
	Effective punctuation	Write a couple of paragraphs – perhaps a description of someone or something – and **try to get in all the punctuation you know**.
	Improving sentences	Take one of the paragraphs you have written above and **rewrite it, with more sentence variety**, as appropriate.
	Using impressive vocabulary	Regularly, consider **learning five new words and their meanings** – words that are impressive and that you might not normally use, e.g. 'stigmatise', 'chasm', 'idyllic'… You then hope you might have the opportunity to use some of them in your exam responses.
P1, Q5/6	Writing to describe	**Plan a description.** The next time, **write a paragraph** from the plan, making the standard as high as you can manage. Try to **write an opening**. Then, another time, **an ending**.
P1, Q5/6	Writing to narrate	**Plan a story.** As with description, the next time **write an opening** (introducing a character, setting, situation…) and, later, **an ending**… and at another time write a brief but revealing extract of **conversation**.
P2, Q5	Writing with a viewpoint	Decide on an issue that interests you, then **repeat the plan/opening/ending practices**.

All of this is not nearly as hard as it looks. But the sooner you start, the better!

Revision checklist

This section offers you a simple way keep a check on the vital elements in this book and to make sure you have revised them all. Tick them off as you complete them.

Paper 1, Section A

Pages	Question	Topic	Workbook complete	Extra practice
4–5		Using evidence to support your ideas		
6–9	P1, Q1	Finding relevant details		
10–15	P1, Q2	Writing about language in literature		
16–21	P1, Q3	Dealing with structure		
22–30	P1, Q4	Character, relationships, themes and settings		

Paper 2, Section A

Pages	Question	Topic	Workbook complete	Extra practice
32–33	P2, Q1	Finding what is true		
34–39	P2, Q2	Dealing with two texts and summarising		
40–45	P2, Q3	Analysing persuasive language		
46–54	P2, Q4	Comparing viewpoints and writers' methods		

Section Bs

Pages	Question	Topic	Workbook complete	Extra practice
56–57		Communicating effectively		
58–61		Organising your writing		
62–65		Vocabulary and crafting		
66–67		Using effective punctuation		
68–69		Improving sentences and grammar		
70–79	P1	Writing to describe		
80–89	P1	Writing to narrate		
90–97	P2	Writing with a viewpoint		

Workbook answers can be found at www.hoddereducation.co.uk/myrevisionnotes/gcse-english-language